VOICED

A Poetry Collection of Light & Hope

AF578164

By Shriya Prasad

Copyright © Shriya Prasad
All Rights Reserved.

This book has been self-published with all reasonable efforts taken to make the material error-free by the author. No part of this book shall be used, reproduced in any manner whatsoever without written permission from the author, except in the case of brief quotations embodied in critical articles and reviews.

The Author of this book is solely responsible and liable for its content including but not limited to the views, representations, descriptions, statements, information, opinions and references ["Content"]. The Content of this book shall not constitute or be construed or deemed to reflect the opinion or expression of the Publisher or Editor. Neither the Publisher nor Editor endorse or approve the Content of this book or guarantee the reliability, accuracy or completeness of the Content published herein and do not make any representations or warranties of any kind, express or implied, including but not limited to the implied warranties of merchantability, fitness for a particular purpose. The Publisher and Editor shall not be liable whatsoever for any errors, omissions, whether such errors or omissions result from negligence, accident, or any other cause or claims for loss or damages of any kind, including without limitation, indirect or consequential loss or damage arising out of use, inability to use, or about the reliability, accuracy or sufficiency of the information contained in this book.

Made with ♥ on the Notion Press Platform
www.notionpress.com

To you, because everyone deserves a little bit of sunshine <3

#QUOTE 1.

"What if we treated people as we do art? No anger, no questions—just acceptance for the unique masterpiece each one of us are."

~ **Shriya Prasad**

LOVE

Someone once asked me, "What does
love mean to you?"
That's when I realized, I didn't
have an answer, until I accepted
you
The warmth of sunlight that awakens
me each morning
The stars that watch me from afar
is you
Zephyr sings to me when I'm unhappy
Thunder claps, when there's no one
else to
Rain clings onto my skin on both
good and bad days
I love the rain, I really do
The truth is, every element of life
is love to me
So, here's my final answer
Dear life, love is about loving you

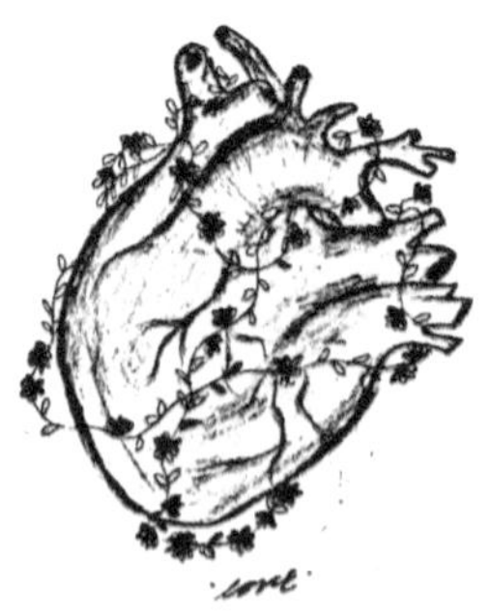

HUMAN

The clouds aren't always stuck in
the sky
They bleed to the ground at
different timelines
But it must be that way sometimes
Otherwise, there would be no rain,
no storm, no life
Different colors of clouds I see
and once again I breathe in relief
Knowing what it's like to be human
Knowing what it's like to feel

WAR

The clouds have descended, making
way for hail to set afoot
I remember trying to understand why
there had to be wars for the world
to evolve
I didn't get why there had to be
pain, hurt, sadness when there was
peace and love to be found
But I end the quarrel to my
judgment, because even if rampage
of waves crash onto each other
The waves will become the sea, the
ocean, the river
I begin to smile; I begin to run
Good will ascend, but sometimes it
takes a war

VOICED

I don't know why we're screaming
despite being so rich and beautiful
We've turned oceans to floods
Trees to dust
Animals to chains
The freedom of birds caged
Wilderness to buildings
Nature should be screaming. Not us.
Humans we're born and we must
Stop demanding for more and save
what soon will be lost

IRIDESCENCE

Sunlight prickles onto my skin
Elixir of prisms compete; there’s no win
The sky adjourns the quarrel
Iridescence is amidst...

#QUOTE 2.

"The sky is never always clear, even after its existence for forever, so how can you expect yourself to walk on a straight path, all the time?"

~ **Shriya Prasad**

DREAMS

"What do you want to be when you grow up?"
That was a question I never could answer
I wanted to sketch the imaginary, travel around the globe, serve humanity
It was a question that I could've answered
If it was, "What will you do when you grow up?" instead
Since there's no single path when there are endless dreams to create and endless dreams to conquer

JUST BREATHE

To me your eyes aren't darkness
To me your smile is so much more
I see a spark buried within you
Raring to be unleashed, ready to open doors
Your voice radiates calmness
But I can see your mind wander
Between dreams to nothingness
Questions to be answered
But you question yourself more...your desires, your abilities
I want to reassure you
You truly are more than what's on the screen
You assume that you're just a shadow
Well, you're the one holding onto yourself from beneath
You're so different in a good way, so beautiful...just breathe

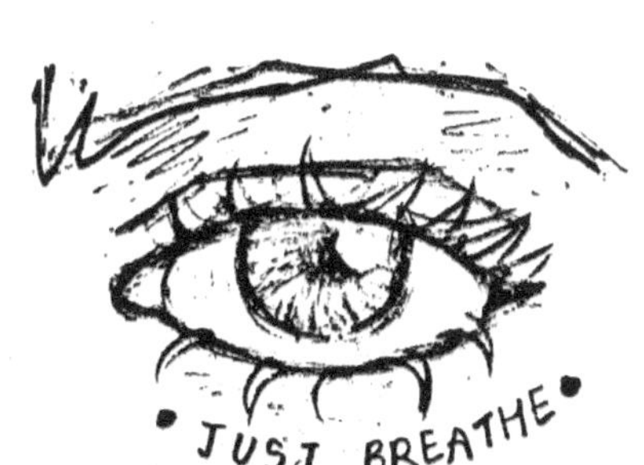

MY WORLD

Pictures and scribbles on white sheets
Ripped on the edges, I peer beneath
It engulfs me within
I walk among trees, stars, it's serene
I smile too soon, I awaken
My fairytale is just a dream

FREEDOM

Some of us don't belong here—we
don't belong here
We don't fit in mediocrity
We can't keep up with the
guidelines set by humanity
Souls scrambling for freedom
Awaiting to be awaken
Immersed within books, music,
anything that screams "escapism"
We're dreamers, dreaming about a
world beyond us
Waiting for the day , where freedom
isn't labeled a cost

#QUOTE 3.

"True love isn't just about sacrificing your life for someone, it's about bringing out the life within them."

~ **Shriya Prasad**

HELLO

Hello? well, I was still
daydreaming
He isn't going to look at me
But I still look at him though
I see us talking and laughing,
planning our futures together
We would get along so well I just
knew, though we never spoke
I memorized his smile, the dimple
on his left check, the glint in his
eye
But I stood away a hundred feet,
who was I?
Would he ever know?
Behind me, I heard a voice, a
familiar tone
Butterflies consummated me
entirely, it was him...
To me he said "Hello"

"Hello?"

THE ONE

She fell first, she gave him a
smile
He looked away, he couldn't meet
her eyes
She listened to songs about love
and beyond
He wrote poems about her even when
she wasn't around
Her dreams became his
His dreams were her only
She was captivated by his smile
But he dreamt about her laughter
To him she was "the one" only...

RIGHT PERSON

I knew the moment you liked me, but
uncertainty brewed itself onto my
head
I finally realized; I'd fallen for
you, but did your feelings wane? Or
did they still hold true?
Distance wedged its way in between,
forcing me to face and say the
truth
The sunsets fade, the stars arise,
but you're still the one on my mind
You're the thought that fills my
days, a vision pure, inked onto
every page
The depth of love, it knows no end,
in every thought, you're still my
friend.
Anticipating the moment where fate
aligns, our hearts together, no
more "goodbyes"
Waiting for the day, it's my "the
end",
"You're mine" I would've finally
said

SOMEBODY

I want someone to look me in the
eye and unravel my thoughts
Underneath the umbrella of stars,
he spins me around
I want someone to go on late-night
drives with our favorite song
With the windows down and our
hearts singing along
I want someone to hold my hand with
laughter and love
In this tapestry of life, our
journeys are one
Yet, this someone I long for, a
figment, it seems
In my delusional mind, a creation
of dreams
But in real life, oh, the prospect
is near
I can't wait to meet you, my heart
whispers, "sincere"

#QUOTE 4.

"Being positive is not a temporary feeling, it's a practice."

~ **Shriya Prasad**

THE HORIZON

If your happiness forever lies on the horizon
And there's always a cup to fill before you allow yourself to breathe
Setting goals isn't a bad thing but relying only on achievements for satisfaction shouldn't be the dream
Yes, you need ambitions and ideas to succeed
But you'd be happy within if you decide to learn what happiness feels like truly

STARDUST

I don't know if you knew
But we're all woven stardust
Our bodies, the same particles
That birth the stars, a cosmic thrust
Isn't it beautiful, this connection?
A calling, perhaps, that we bear
A fraction of the world within us
The essence of the universe, that we share

COLOR

The sky isn't black or blue
It's transparent and keeps
reflecting different shades of the
ocean onto me and you
If the sky didn't switch color or
didn't project any color at all
There would be no life, no change,
nothing to see, no dusk or dawn
So, I'm trying to say, try new
things, change yourself, choose the
best color on the palette
A better person, the best version
of yourself

LETTERS

I find Languages intricate but intriguing
Sounds to words, words to sentences, sentences to lessons, lessons with meaning
People didn't discover languages, they created them
Strung together letters to convey thoughts, ideas and feelings
The human mind is truly an endless reservoir of creativity
Each day, more is discovered on this limitless universe upon which we are standing
Languages are the beginning what's more to create, will forever be an open ending

MOMENT

The birds fly over the horizon, "In union" some would say
But I see one dive past the rest, taking flight towards the other way
None of the others could dare but this one drew a different line on the blue
Bringing life to the sky today, that's what I want to do
I want to choose my ride with every step I take
I know some roads might not be the best ones
But it's okay to make a mistake
I'd rather just live right now
Instead of saying tomorrow is the perfect one
Because there's no guarantee that I'll get the chance to say, "I made it today" if there won't come one

#QUOTE 5.

"Time does fly, just like a plane but you can slow it down and waver right there, by cherishing every kind of cloud you glide through in the sky."

~ **Shriya Prasad**

A WINDY DAY

I close my eyes, as I sit on the passenger seat
The wind hits my face, hitting every inch of me
Nostalgia slams, flashes of images run by taping themselves onto me
Suddenly I'm young on the swing, just me
I launch myself higher and higher just to feel the wind's company
The scene shifts, I see the sun diving into the ocean, the waves clutching it from beneath
All of a sudden, it's quiet, I open my eyes
The wind has stopped, creating yet another memory

SOUL FRIEND

Many walk in and out of each one's life
Often the reason said is, clash, growth or distance
But most importantly, people do change
Sometimes, this brings people closer if they believe that it's worth
But other times this pushes people apart if they believe, it won't work
I believe the people who put the effort to stay despite change are the ones meant to be present
To those ones, I feel immense gratitude because you really are my greatest present

AN ODE OF THANKS

She was the first one to open her arms to me
She became my shadow when I lost a part of me
She was never a patient person, but she listened to me
Though I'd never thank her for putting me back on my feet
Then there came our miscommunications that she'd be forced to oversee
I wouldn't say sorry because I assumed she should be the one to apologize to me
Little did I know she was the one putting herself behind me
I know it's late to say "thank you"
But I'd like to, so here's me
Dear mom, thank you for being the one person
The only person I'll ever need

KITES

Children carry their kites like parents once hold the hands of their children
With the guidance of a string, the kite flies further and further into the sky
Then finally the time comes...the time comes for the kite to fly away high
For the string to let loose, to say goodbye
Children are the kites, parents are the strings to their lives

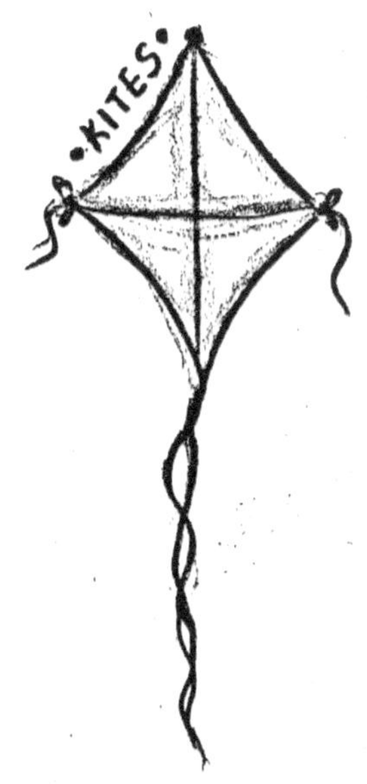

FOREVER FRIENDS

Rivers will flow, seasons will
change
Talks will be forgotten, memories
will fade
It's beautiful to watch people grow
and evolve into different
individuals and not grow apart
Time, the alchemy for bonds to
ascend
Laughter, an enduring cure; forever
a friend

ACCEPTANCE

I wanted to have another conversation
Hear her ringing laughter
Hold her hand again, Give her another hug
Smile lines on her face, she had the most though she was the one to see the worst
A mother of two, family to all
That's my dear grandmother
She deserves the world; she deserves it all
I want to keep laughing with her
I want to keep talking to her
But I know no one’s here forever
But I'll smile at our memories because she is a part of me; I’ll never forget her

#QUOTE 6.

"It's alright to be the only star in the night of rightness, even if the world around you prefers to choose the shadows."

~ **Shriya Prasad**

NIGHT SKIES

There's something special about the night sky
There's nothing to see except for the moon; the lighting knight
There's nothing to see, yet I gaze up in awe
Everyone adores the moon and stars
But that wouldn't be special if not for the hold of the dark sky
That's sacrifice
Those are the hidden gems, the selfless people,
The ones who give and give and give
But never receive—never receive the appreciation
There's so many of these night skies around us
To some you are one too
If a kind word or a smile could make one's day
Just be kind, would you?

#QUOTE 7.

"It's true that beauty isn't just confined to physical attributes...roses loose their petals too."

~ **Shriya Prasad**

YOU

It's true if you want to love
someone else you must first love
yourself
No one should be the reason for
your happiness unless the first
reason is you
If you want to grasp every single
moment of life, you've got let
yourself heal you
If you want to be happy in your
skin, you must allow yourself to
accept you
You can jot down a hundred reasons
on why you should hate yourself,
but master forgiveness, just
forgive you
If there's greater good, you want
to give and share to the world
The first thing you can do for the
better is see the good within you

THE PERFECT WAVE

I've never seen a perfect wave,
I doubt I ever will
Even the sea knows that you don't
need perfection to be the version
you envision
It's alright to be wild and free
it's alright to break the chains
and lose the key
I know the sea agrees with me

#QUOTE 8.

"In the quiet cocoon of patience,
the caterpillar dreams
metamorphosing into winged colors
of the butterfly: a testament of
hope & perseverance."

~ **Shriya Prasad**

JOURNEY

I hate this, this version of me,
that's trapped in my mind, unable
to be free
What if this person that I've
become is the person I'm meant to
be?
I don't know what I did to deserve
this, but I do know the mistake was
never mine
I take a deep breathe, I must allow
change, if I want to take another
stride
It's not an instant metamorphosis,
but a journey, where resilience
must abide
A day will come, when the wait is
over, the day will come, where I
learn to smile

MY HEART

My heart; a canvas painted with
dreams
Stories I envision, there's so much
to see
So much to explore, so much to find
Plethora of thoughts stuck on my
mind
Wondering where life's journey will
lead
In 10 years of time, where would I
be?
Excitement builds for what's meant
to be
Anticipating the day when I'm
finally free

NAVIGATION

The currents will keep changing but
that's because you are on the ship
called "Life"
Just keep sailing, I promise you,
you'll navigate through
You're a sailor, not the one to
drown
You're somebody who can swim
through the ocean, even on days
where there's no clear sky or rope
Just hold on
You were born here not to fight,
but to learn to survive

#QUOTE 9.

"In life's melody, rain brings
challenges and growth harmonizes.
But through the storms, flowers
bloom, and through the clouds,
light pierces through."

Be brave; your sunshine awaits
Hold on; it's worth the wait...

~ **Shriya Prasad**

I MADE IT

I reminisce about the day, where I
look back and say, "Hey, I made it"
but no, I'm not there yet
I still have hurdles in my way, I
have this pressing feeling of
wanting to end today
With a skip to the future, but no,
would I be satisfied? Would I learn
from my mistakes?
I question my purpose, my purpose
in life
I know that's something to be
created, not something to find
I think, I think, I think, my
present and delusional mind fight
But I keep quiet, I stick to my
word
I'll work towards something,
something worth
Even if it means I must take an
eternity's oath

SURVIVAL

Like the rhyme about the spider
Many a time, rain mess up their webs
But a glistened web sparkles with dew drops the next morning,
because the spider weaves its web again
I don't see determination as knowing they'll succeed
But I see determination as being able to do something despite calamities
Spiders weave their webs
Oblivious of upcoming rain
And once their homes are destroyed
They start weaving again

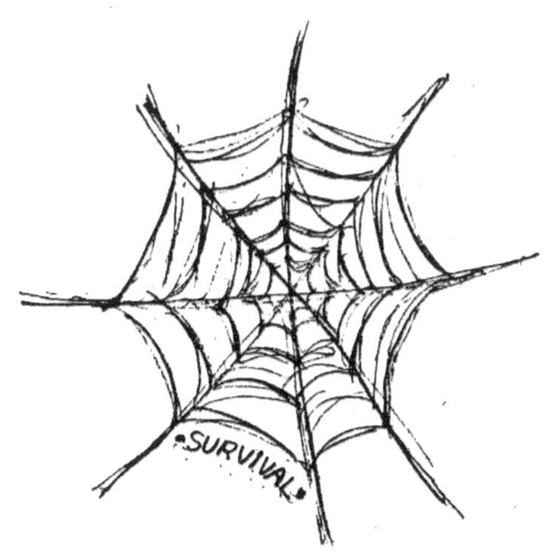

GROWING UP

That diary of mine, ripped and torn
Pages of words, I didn't deserve
I glance back, wondering what I'll find
But I remind myself every time
That every flower doesn't bloom the same
But each one's beauty is its claim
That's something that I'll learn to believe
Though my past decides to scream
With rips and tears, my diary in hand
A symbol of growth, where I now stand

LIMITLESS

The sky's the limit, they say
No, the sky is just the beginning,
I look away
There's hope, love, and answers to
seek
Past, future, and present to live
in between
Ceaseless wonder and ideas to
portray
Lies, hatred, armouring ourselves,
keeping defeat at bay
The stars that I want to meet
someday
I'm awake, waiting to reach you one
day
I tell myself again and again
Life is boundless, just don't seal
the gate

#QUOTE 10.

"Life is like a boat, it sways up and down and sometimes it sinks but you've got to swim back up to see the light again, waiting for you above..."

~ **Shriya Prasad**

ABOUT THE AUTHOR

Meet Shriya Prasad, the teenage dynamo behind the pen and positivity! Hailing from the vibrant land of India, this high schooler has turned her passion for words and art into a delightful illustration of poems and quotes. Her book reflects not just her literary talent but also her profound understanding of the power of words.

When asked about her hobbies, she will tell you she loves animals almost as much as she loves teasing her friends. So, if you are in for a good laugh and a splash of positivity, she is your go-to person!
With this book, Shriya is on a mission to sprinkle a bit of sunshine onto the world. If her poems don't make you smile, just imagine her serenading a cat with her guitar - because yes, that's probably happening too!

You can also catch her dishing out inspiration on her Instagram page, where she goes by the handle: @shriyawritesofficial. Cheers to this teen making the world brighter, one quote at a time!

Use your phone camera to scan this QR code to access links where you can leave reviews and follow shriya!

www.ingramcontent.com/pod-product-compliance
Lightning Source LLC
La Vergne TN
LVHW091237150826
845673LV00003B/1177

* 9 7 9 8 8 9 2 3 3 8 2 0 2 *